For the Love of Our Daughters:

An Adoption Journey

Patti Janco

No part of this publication may be reproduced or transmitted in any form or by any means, electronic or mechanical, without permission in writing from the author.

This book is dedicated with special thanks and love to my husband and best friend, Gary. When we found ourselves in the depths of hell, you took my hand and we continued to walk forward, one step at a time.

Gratitudes

Much thanks to my friends (you know who you are) who encouraged me to finally write this book. Your encouragement has led me to resolve issues and heal in ways I was unaware needed healing.

With unending appreciation for my sisters, Kathy and Lorene, who were and still are always there for me. Thank you for sharing this life-long family journey. Your love and support has meant the world to me.

To my friend and literary advisor, Beth Hanggeli, whose advice, editing skills, encouragement and support were instrumental in the final production of this book.

To our daughters, Carrie and Maria, who were the driving force and purpose of this journey. It was often a long and challenging road, but was always driven by love. As your parents, we did the very best we could.

In Loving Memory of my parents with eternal gratitude, for my Mother, who was always there for me.

"I miss you, Mom. I miss you every day of my life."

<u>For My Parents</u>
When you are gone,
I will not remember
What you bought for my 13th birthday,
How you baked my favorite cookies,
Or what you gave me for Christmas in 1972.
I won't remember my first bike
Or how we ever made it through my childhood.
However----
There are a few things I will remember
Like, the year you gave me the sun.
A gift---without price tag,
impossible to hold,
unable to be solely owned.
But it was a gift of time and sharing.
A gift made of---
seashells and sandcastles
long morning walks
palm trees, sailboats
and sunsets.
We spent summers---
floating lazily on the water
soaking up the sun
chasing the seagulls
capturing memories
living a dream.
You started me on a journey of a lifetime.
A journey that would carry me to many times
and many places, eternally in search of the sun.
Now though,
I must pause----
While I have the chance,
And Thank You
Not only for showing me the sun,
But more so for sharing it.
And---one day---
When you are gone,
I will think of you—
Whenever I look toward the Sun.

For those who are called
to follow the path through adoption…
Let your heart push the fears away.

Chapter 1

My husband Gary and I both grew up in a small town in Ohio during the '60s, when marriages lasted a lifetime and family values were prevalent, no matter what one's religious affiliation might be. We were raised with high expectations by parents who experienced the Great Depression and all the lessons it taught to that generation.

Our introduction during our first week of the 9th grade began our life together as best friends and eventually soulmates for life when we married in the Fall of 1975. During the eight years that followed, we did a lot of volunteer work with Big Brothers Big Sisters and became aware of the numbers of children all over the world in need of adoptive homes. It was during this time that the dream to provide a home for a child or children in need took root.

In August of 1983, Gary and I relocated from our small hometown in Ohio to the northeast Florida area, where we purchased over an acre of raw land. We cleared trees, learned to use an old-fashioned sickle and leveled the terrain with the help of our 15-year-old nephew. We learned about septic tanks, deep drilled wells and everything it took to live peacefully in our rural environment. Little did we realize at the time that it would require years of clearing, burning, tree removal and landscaping. After years of living in the city with sewers, water, paved roads, and streetlights, we felt like pioneers in a new land. It turned out that this was one of the best decisions we would ever make.

We fell in love with our rural area. It was abundant with nature and life was good. We enjoyed watching deer, fox, bunnies, eagles, owls and a wide variety of other wildlife. We loved being close to the beach with dolphins, whales, manatees, crabs and sea birds. We lived a simple, peaceful life that was perfect for raising a family.

As we cleared our land by hand, we contemplated building our family through local adoption. We contacted several agencies in the city and learned that the chance of adopting a baby was not possible, which was fine with us. We preferred a child from 3-5 years of age. However, the waiting list for a child in that age range was anywhere from 5-8 years.

We began to believe there were few children in our country in need of being adopted, but that was far from the truth. One social worker assured us that there was a need, but the backlog was so great that children were falling through the many cracks in the system. There were not enough social workers to address the needs of children trapped in the foster care system. In addition, laws at the time required biological parents to willingly sign their parental rights away and few were willing to do that. Due to this law, many children were hopelessly trapped in the foster care system, growing up in foster homes instead of with permanent families, either biological or adoptive.

This information gave us much to think about and contemplate. We didn't want to see a child wait for years to be adopted and we didn't want to wait that long to build our family. Surely, there were children somewhere who needed a chance for a good life. Those were the thoughts that finally led us to international adoption.

It all began with 1 1/3 acres of woods and brush.

Chapter 2

In November of 1983, we decided to submit an application to an international adoption agency. This began our worldly search for what we hoped would eventually lead us to a daughter. We had requested a girl, as we knew there was an abundance of girls available. Girls in other cultures were more likely to be surrendered for adoption than the coveted males. The idea that males were preferred and females unwanted was a sad fact that settled us on wanting and requesting a girl.

The paperwork required for adoption was extensive and took months to complete. Our extended families were required to write letters of recommendation in support of the adoption. We were also subjected to doctor visits, physicals, blood tests, financial investigations, finger printing for numerous database searches, psychological interviews, employer questionnaires, background checks, home studies, various meetings and an endless trail of other miscellaneous paperwork.

There were decisions to be made as to which countries to submit our adoption application. We had chosen Korea as our first choice, followed by the Philippines. Foreign countries open and close themselves to adoptions at will. This can happen when there is a change in the government, or when they decide to close and increase their adoption fees upon re-opening. As luck would have it, our countries of choice both closed just as we were prepared to submit our paperwork.

A few months later, the country of Honduras opened for the first time and we were given the opportunity to be the first test case through that country. This choice would require us to travel, once we were matched with our child. It was a requirement of Honduras to establish temporary residency in order to adopt.

While we waited for a phone call with a child placement from the adoption agency, we decorated a little girl's room, researched girls' names and made plans for the great life our little family would enjoy. We also continued to clear land and create a backyard play area.

On October 22, 1984, we received a call asking if we would accept a little girl who was 18 months old. We had requested a child age 2-5 years, so this age was good. We accepted her "sight unseen" and waited for her photo to arrive.

We felt so blessed, and a week later our hearts wrapped around the prettiest little girl with a head full of brown hair and big, sad, brown eyes. She didn't look very thrilled with having her photo taken, but we were thrilled to have an image to attach our hearts to.

Additional paperwork and requests for financial fees arrived with the photo, and we set about converting her Honduran name "Carolina" and Americanizing it to "Caroline." We would call her "Carrie." This photo was duplicated and sent to relatives far and wide. So now, there were grandparents, aunts, uncles, cousins and friends all excited because she was now "real," with a photo, a name and now, a home.

The next surprise in our lives came a month later when we learned about Carrie's younger sister, who was under a year old and was also available for adoption. We were told she had a tropical illness and had not been cleared for adoption at the same time as Carrie. Again, "sight unseen," we agreed to adopt the sister, who would be named "Maria." We were given no additional information about her and there would be

For the Love of Our Daughters

no photo forthcoming, but the commitment to keep two sisters together never allowed us to waiver for a moment.

I have two wonderful sisters myself who have been my companions and friends on this trip through life, and I knew I would never be able to walk away from separating these sisters and still live with myself. The only problem was that we were $2,000 short of the fees needed to adopt both children. What a dilemma!

It took all the money we had saved for a down payment on building a home, plus a monetary gift from my parents, who agreed that these two sisters could not be separated. Now this adoption became a real extended family affair and we were blessed with so much support, both financially and emotionally.

Written while waiting for the girls

Somewhere faraway in this world,
There waits for us two little girls.
Though their skin is darker than mine,
Look a bit closer and you will find.
They're very much like you and me,
Just needing love to set them free.
Perhaps they are that pot of gold,
At the rainbow's end - ours to hold.
And even now as we await,
Anxious, Impatient but full of faith.
One day we'll have our little ones
To share our life beneath the sun.
Although it may take a while,
Hard luck and many lonely miles.
But in the end—
Honduras Smiles.

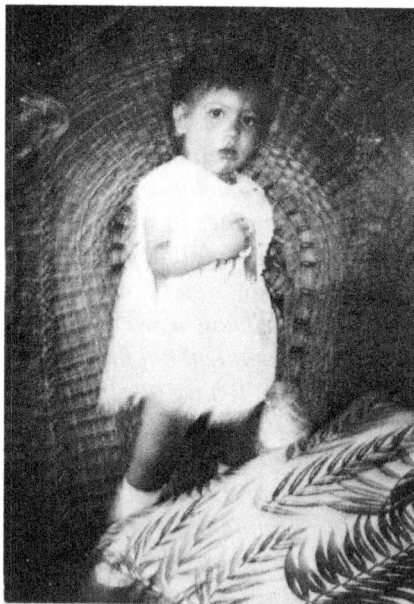

First photo of Carrie

Chapter 3

After learning about and accepting Maria in addition to Carrie, we prepared for our first trip to Honduras. We continued to fill out additional paperwork and learned that over $10,000 in partial fees would have to be paid in cash upon arrival in Honduras. I have no idea, as I write this now, why a red flag of fear did not rise for this dangerous request, but we were on a mission to save two baby girls who desperately needed us and we could not be deterred or frightened away. Many children in Honduras are not in good health and their mortality rate is very high, so time was of the essence. We were committed, and that carried for us a heavy sense of responsibility for their lives and their wellbeing.

During the time we pursued this adoption, there was a great deal of civil unrest in Honduras and through much of Central America. There were rumors of death squads killing and torturing civilians. The Nicaraguan rebels were trying to overthrow their Sandinista government. The United Sates became involved in this with some type of military support. Central American countries opposed the U.S. intervention and Americans fell out of favor. This was the Iran-Contra era and escalating involvement by the U.S. would lead to Honduras being forced into acting as the staging ground for the U.S.-backed covert war against communism. I say all of this only to show how dangerous it became for any Americans to be in Honduras, let alone ones carrying huge amounts of cash.

While we prepared for our own odyssey and adventure to Honduras to see the girls, we gathered small gifts which our agency said were necessary at times to open government-type doors in the adoption. We also collected toys and clothes for our children, as well as any others we would encounter. With this country being so poor, we felt we could help in other ways. We couldn't adopt all the children in need, but maybe we could improve some of their lives in some small way.

We purchased money belts to carry the required cash and fees we would need to pay, but learned that it was not a good idea to have this money that easily removed. So, we divided the money between us, placed it in Ziploc bags, and duct-taped it to our abdomen and backs.

We took unpaid leave from our employers for three weeks, which further worried us for our financial future and the ability to support our little family. Back in our younger days, we were not easily scared or deterred from what we felt was the right thing to do and at that time, this all just felt right. Of course, from where I stand today, 34 years later, I am amazed at how young and naïve we really were. But life was still an adventure then and we really hadn't lived long enough to develop the fears that would come to us here in our later years. As we look back now, we wonder how we had the nerve to do all that we did.

On December 5, 1984, my sister Kathy drove us to the airport and we were on our way to Miami, where we would change planes to San Pedro Sula, Honduras. It would be a full day of travel, layovers and delays, but our excitement and anticipation of meeting our daughters for the first time carried us through.

Upon landing in Miami, we were directed to the far end of the airport where we had several hours to wait for our final flight to San Pedro. It was a deserted area, very quiet and with little activity. There was an old plane at the end of the tarmac that appeared as though it was being restored. There were cracks in one of the passenger windows, a small piece of the tail was missing, there was rust on the wing, and what appeared to be a low or flat tire under the nose of the plane. We joked and laughed about what a rust bucket it looked like and that it was probably going to be taken to the junk yard after it was stripped for salvageable parts. Little did we know at the time that this was the Tan Sasha plane that would take us roughly and uncertainly to our destination in Honduras.

The plane ride was nerve-wracking and terrifying. The plane was old inside, with doors missing on some of the overhead bins, and it shook threateningly on takeoff as if the nuts and bolts holding it together were coming apart. We didn't know there would be additional landing and takeoffs, as the plane made an unscheduled stop in an unnamed country where we were told not to stand up or attempt to get off the plane. This mystery country was supposedly closed to anyone not authorized to arrive, and our plane was immediately surrounded by soldiers with military tanks and machine guns. Welcome to the way of life in a Central American country. We were only just beginning to miss the good old USA.

During our time in Honduras, it was evident that Honduras was a country of contrasts. As we flew over lush tropical forests and endless green sugar cane, coffee and banana plantations, the view was breathtaking. Mayan ruins spoke of a time gone by when that creative civilization built amazing temples and settlements, and then disappeared. Tall stone monuments with carved hieroglyphics buried in the rainforests near the Guatemalan border were, and are today, a testament to an ancient civilization dedicated to ceremony.

Honduras has always been known to have the world's highest murder rates and high levels of sexual violence against women, starting at very young ages. A mortician in San Pedro Sula, where the girls were born, once said, "Satan himself lives here. People here kill people like they are nothing more than chickens."

Citizens of Honduras have always lived in extreme poverty. Water quality has always been poor and housing deplorable. Our children came from a cardboard city in the mountains surrounding the city of San Pedro Sula. Disease and death were rampant due to filthy living conditions, and not many survived to an elderly age.

During our time in San Pedro Sula, we were unnerved by how young the military soldiers were who carried guns throughout the city streets. They could and did use their authority to stop us, inquire about our American presence, confiscate our passports, detain us, and verify our visas. These were very nerve-wracking and fearful times.

Yes, Honduras is a country of contrasts, for sure. Beautiful scenery and a heartbreaking life for children, as we realized one day while having lunch with our lawyers in a restaurant. Looking in the window was a filthy group of young faces, ages three to teens, peering longingly at our plates with their hands extended, begging for food. Our reaction was to want to feed them, which our lawyers quickly and vehemently stopped us from doing.

They explained that these were the homeless street children that lived in groups. They begged and stole from wherever and whoever they could in order to survive. Feeding or acknowledging them in any way would open us up to their crimes. This broke our hearts, as we realized then that our children could have ended up with this type of life. It was such a sad and heartbreaking day when we were forced to ignore those needy children.

When we finally arrived at the airport in San Pedro, there was an English-speaking interpreter sent by the Honduran lawyers to assist us through customs and deliver us safely to the proper hotel. There we were to meet with our adoption lawyers who were not bilingual, so the interpreter was a very welcome addition, despite the extra fees.

Upon arrival at the hotel, we met with the lawyers and paid our fees. There was no receipt given. We had to trust that these lawyers would be honest and not demand more than we had already given them. We had no proof that this money had exchanged hands, and I hoped the interpreter would serve as a witness in our favor if the need would arise.

A short time after our exchange with the lawyers, Carrie was brought and introduced to us. She was very shy, and spent her time repeatedly folding and unfolding a small towel. We tried to engage her with the toys we brought, but she was more interested in folding and unfolding her towel. Our interpreter explained that she was fostered in the lawyer's home by their maid who cleaned all day, and Carrie was imitating her. It made us feel bad that this almost two-year-old was subjected to live as a worker rather than the playful life of a toddler.

Once Carrie was comfortable with us, the lawyers left and went to get Maria, who had been kept in a different foster home. Upon their return, Carrie took one look at her sister, yelled "Mia" and ran to throw her arms around her. The lawyers were surprised that Carrie seemed to remember her sister. They had been separated for several months in different foster care situations; eventually, we would come to learn the story of their early lives.

One of the first photos of Maria

Chapter 4

Seeing Carrie for the first time, she appeared to be healthy, although she was only being fed powdered milk, and all of that was passing directly through her system. She was almost two years old, weighed just under 20 lbs. and was 29" tall. The age estimate given to us stateside was different for both girls when we arrived in Honduras. Carrie was not a happy child and she cried a lot for no apparent reason.

The birth mother was said to be only 13 years old when Carrie was born and 14 when Maria came along. Their father was a plantation worker who traveled from plantation to plantation, picking crops of coffee and bananas. The parents never married, probably because the birth mother was so young and the father was around 19.

Upon returning home after some migrant work in another area, the father was informed that the birth mother had tired of waiting and ran off across the mountains to Guatemala to be with another man. She left the babies alone in the mountains with no food or anyone to care for them. When they were found, they were malnourished and seriously ill. They were taken to the home of their paternal grandmother, who was ill herself and could no longer care for them. It was then that the father brought them down into the city to surrender them for adoption.

Because the mother ran off and was not available to sign the children off for adoption, we chose to go to the expense of searching for her. When she could not be located, we placed notices in the newspapers throughout Honduras and Guatemala, looking for her. According to government regulations, if she did not come forward within 30 days, her parental rights would be permanently terminated. We did this with heavy hearts, knowing she could come forward and we could lose the children. But there was no way we were going to take these children out of the country if the birth mother, a mere child herself, came forward and wanted them back.

The birth father and relatives who still may have had contact with her were also notified, so that all avenues were taken to preserve her parental rights. Despite these steps, she failed to come forward. Perhaps even at her young age, she knew that she did not have what it would take to be a mother, and this was her best way out.

We have never moved from where we live today. The lawyers and Honduran authorities knew of our location, but we have never heard anything further.

♡

Maria was almost a year old when she was brought to us. The adoption agency had told us she was ill and could not be cleared for adoption. At almost a year old, she was 26" long and weighed just under 12 lbs. We would come to find out that she was severely malnourished.

The doctors in Honduras predicted that Maria would not have lived another six months in her native country. Infant death rates in Honduras were and still are very high. We would come to learn that the original plan was to institutionalize her and not seek adoptive parents. Rumor was that perspective adoptive parents from a European country had turned her down. While they were in a doctor's office deciding not to take her, a black lady overheard them talking, and offered to take her as a foster parent and nurse her along with her own infant. The doctors there felt this was probably what saved her life and made her healthy enough to try again to be adopted. If not for the loving kindness of that special angel who nursed Maria with her own life-saving milk, Maria would have perished.

When we first saw Maria in our hotel, she was covered in what would soon be diagnosed as scabies, and it needed to be treated. It was only through the grace of God that neither Gary, I, nor Carrie became infested. The treatment for scabies required Maria to be covered from head to toe for a full 24 hours in a toxic medication that would kill the bugs and eventually restore her skin to a healthy, natural state. The medication smelled awful and Maria cried as we followed the instructions.

The next day, we bathed Maria, removing the layer of medication, and took her to the doctor to be checked over. The doctor had been trained in the States, and felt he needed to give us his honest opinion about Maria and her future. He felt there was a high chance that Maria might never walk, talk or learn like other children, since she was currently functioning on a three-month-old level. He advised us to think long and hard about the years ahead and to consider turning down her placement with us. We were not technically obligated to take her at that point, and I am sure he was trying to be completely honest with his opinion for our sake. However, we never considered this option. We were totally committed to our girls, and so we chose to ignore his advice.

Chapter 5

The early days after our arrival in Honduras were a sleepless blur of challenges. We were in a strange country in a dilapidated hotel that was supposedly the best, with no provisions or ability to care for and feed Carrie and Maria. Fortunately, our adoption agency stepped in, and we were offered the opportunity to rent a room from a local Honduran dentist and his wife who spoke English. At their house, we had the conveniences of a home with appliances, better accommodations for the children, and other adoptive families from the United States and other countries to socialize with and share experiences. These other families were also working with our agency and lawyers to secure the adoption of their children.

On December 6, 1984, we met with our lawyers and the girls' birth father to sign the adoption papers. He was of Mestizo Indian descent, very tall and slender. A poor migrant worker, he traveled the country from plantation to plantation in search of work and could no longer find anyone to care for the girls. He was relieved to sign the papers, and could then return to finding work to support himself and his ill mother.

In the days that followed, we went shopping in the market, played with the other families and went to many doctor appointments in an effort to get the children well. We visited the pharmacy often to purchase prescription vitamins and medications for both girls. Maria was very weak and unable to even sit up on her own without being propped up by a pillow. We were concerned for her future development and wanted to do everything possible to get her well enough to eventually travel home to Florida.

Carrie was experiencing a lot of intestinal issues. All the food and milk she consumed went right through her. This meant she was not getting the nutrition she desperately needed to grow and develop properly. She cried constantly for no apparent reason and we were concerned with her physical, mental and emotional state. She didn't play like other children and it concerned us that she acted more like an adult than a two-year-old toddler.

On December 14th, we had a very important adoption meeting with our lawyers and some government officials in the capital city of Tegucigalpa. Our lawyers loaded several families in an old van for the four-hour drive on treacherous, unpaved roads through the mountains. There were no seatbelts or car seats in this old van for the children so we each had a tight hold on the girls, as the lawyer was also a dangerous and reckless driver. At one point, the van hit a wide crevice in the dirt road, and threw us all forward and onto the floor. We were all terrified, and the children were screaming. This finally convinced the lawyer to slow his erratic driving. The children were unhurt, but the adults suffered various injuries trying to protect the children that would stay with us for weeks.

Upon arrival in Tegucigalpa, we were directed into the office of a government official who collected additional fees from us. We were also directed by the lawyers to distribute the gifts that we were instructed to purchase back in the U.S. and bring with us to Honduras. After gifts of chocolates and small items were given out in several offices, we were placed in a meeting room to wait for the official who would sign and approve our adoption application papers. This meeting lasted about four minutes after the four-hour drive to get there. We then returned to San Pedro along the same treacherous route. We were sore and exhausted, but grateful to have this trip behind us.

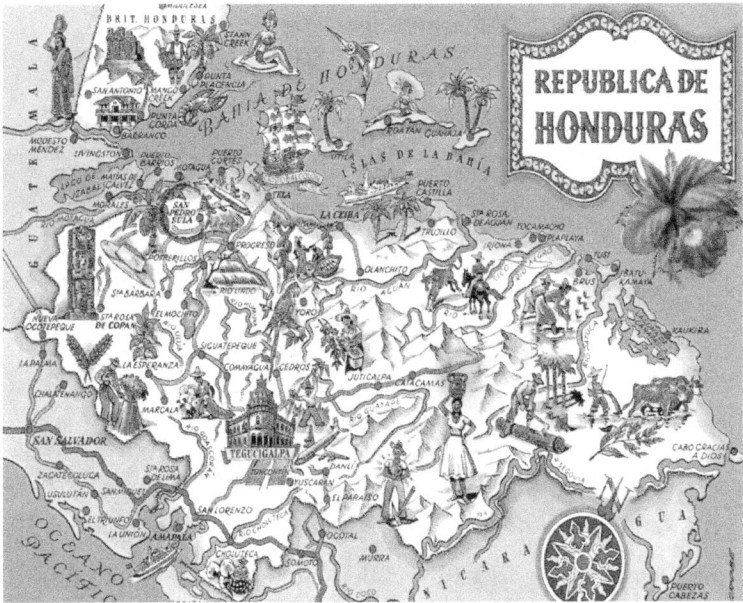

San Pedro Sula is located in the northwest area of Honduras

Chapter 6

As we waited for all the Honduran adoption paperwork to process, we were cautioned that the Christmas holidays would probably delay the adoption process. Chances were good that the government offices would soon close, since the celebration could last for three weeks.

It seemed that few people were working, and the streets were crowded with people drinking and celebrating. Since it seemed to be a dangerous time for us, we rarely ventured out and about in the interest of safety. The one day we did go out to shop for supplies, the military soldiers were everywhere. We walked along carrying the girls, getting more nervous because we were unsure of what all the activity and unrest was about.

Suddenly, a loud gunshot rang out and we frantically ducked into a storefront, where we watched a military truck pass by throwing firecrackers out into the street, followed by Santa throwing candy to the crowds. This was a sort of holiday celebration, not a gun going off or a military maneuver. How we wished we were back in our own country, where we knew what to expect and could feel safe again!

As luck would have it, our visas were close to expiring and there was no chance our adoption would make it through the government approval before the new year. Our original dream of being home with the girls for Christmas had no chance of happening. We would be forced to return to the U.S. without them and wait to come back. This created the added expense of placing them in private foster care and we did not have that extra money. So, with heavy hearts, we returned to our jobs to collect holiday bonus pay and work extra hours to pay for this foster care.

The journey back home was terribly sad and filled with great anxiety. We could only hope and pray the best foster home had been chosen, and the girls would get all the medications and vitamins we purchased for them to be given in our absence. With the foster mother being poor with children of her own, we feared the vitamins would be distributed among all the children, even though they were solely intended for Carrie and Maria.

Chapter 7

The time between our return to the States and the call to return to Honduras passed slowly. It was during this time that I learned my job would be coming to an end in the new year. The company was eliminating jobs and I was in the crosshairs. We worked as much overtime as our jobs permitted and any side chores we could to earn extra money. We continued to clear the raw land we had purchased to make a safe play area for when the girls came home. We were always exhausted and always worried for their wellbeing.

The call that we expected, directing our return for the girls, didn't come as promised in January. Time dragged on, and we couldn't help but wonder and worry about the hold-up and why it was taking longer. The adoption agency assured us that it was being worked on, but every additional week the girls remained in foster care was another expense we were not expecting. It was also another week that we were not sure if they were being fed enough or given their medications and vitamins. It was a time of high anxiety and endless worries.

When the call finally came in early February to return to Honduras, we again purchased the recommended gifts and strapped thousands of dollars in cash to our bodies for the lawyers, the foster care fee and our daily expenses. We arranged to rent our old room from the dentist and felt relieved that we would be in familiar surroundings, where we felt the safest. We secured our visas and looked forward to the last foreign leg of this adoption adventure.

Upon returning to San Pedro Sula, we were taken to the foster home to be reunited with our children and pass out the gifts we brought for the foster mother and her children. As the foster mother thanked us for the gifts, she grabbed my arm and asked to speak with us privately. She was very distraught as she explained to us that her 12-year-old daughter was in extreme danger. She was becoming a sexual target, at her young age, for men who were hanging out in front of their home. These men were trying to lure her daughter into going with them. She assured us that her daughter would cook, clean and help with our children if we would take her home with us.

She was willing to give her child up, rather than have her continue to live with her in Honduras. We explained, as kindly as we could, the many legal reasons that made this impossible. It was so hard to walk away as the mother was begging and pleading with us to save her daughter by taking her with us.

We paid the foster fees in cash and returned to our rented room, where we would spend the next few days completing more paperwork and playing with the girls.

Carrie and Maria both seemed to have gained a bit of weight while we were gone and we were greatly relieved. Carrie, though, continued to cry constantly and we could not figure out why. Maria looked more bright-eyed, although the size and shape of her head began to concern me. We recalled that the birth father had a large head, so we felt it was probably due to her Indian heritage.

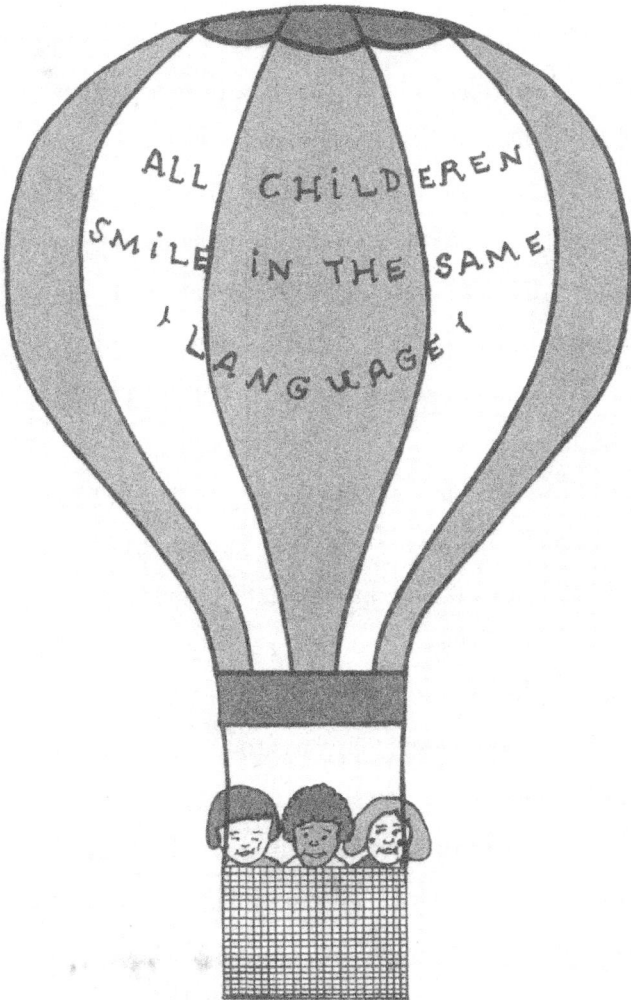

Our Adoption Announcement

Chapter 8

The final leg of our journey in Honduras would take us back to the capital city of Tegucigalpa, where we would go to the American Embassy to obtain the final paperwork required for the girls to enter the U.S. This meant another four-hour drive with the lawyer over the same treacherous roads as before. We were scheduled to leave in the early morning, while it was still dark. This plan allowed us ample time to stop at the Embassy and make our flight back to the States all in one day.

The girls slept most of the way, while we tried to keep a tight hold on them over roads with large holes and cracks that allowed a view straight down into steep ravines. The dark was a blessing in that we couldn't actually see these life-threatening conditions, but we also had no idea when the jarring conditions would throw us around inside the van or possibly dump us over the steep cliffs. At some points, the road had washed out, opening huge cracks to the depths below. I promised I would never again complain about the dirt road we lived on in Florida.

When we arrived in Tegucigalpa, the lawyer delivered us to our hotel and helped us check in. He planned to run some errands and return shortly. We went to the room and put the girls down for a nap as they were tired, crying and hungry. We also were exhausted and crashed ourselves for a few hours.

We waited and waited for the lawyer to return to take us to the Embassy. As darkness fell and he didn't return, we put in a long-distance call to our adoption agency. We explained what was happening and they advised us to sit tight. In the meantime, we took the girls and went out in search of food for them. Carrie was now eating solid foods and everything would go right through her system, so I knew her body was not absorbing the vitamins and nutrients she needed. Maria was on powdered milk and we had no way of getting clean, boiled water in our hotel room. Where on earth was our lawyer? I wondered.

I went down to the hotel kitchen and explained my need for boiled water as best I could with my limited Spanish. The kitchen staff said they would need a $5 donation for the water. I had no choice but to pay it, as Maria was hungry and screaming. I couldn't believe they would charge me to be able to feed one of their own, but was relieved to pay it and get Maria fed. Once Carrie saw Maria's bottle, she began to cry with hunger. So, out to the streets we went in search of food for them, against our better judgment. At a small store, we were able to get some milk and bread for Carrie, along with some peanut butter. We then returned to the hotel to wait.

When we entered our hotel room, we realized that someone had been in our room and had gone through our things. There was some change missing and one of the kids' toys, but everything else seemed to be there. We would later discover, at a most inconvenient time, that the diapers we brought for our trip home were also gone.

We slept very little that night. We were in a strange city, we knew no one and our lawyer was still missing. We were scared and worried. We didn't know what was going on or what we should do. We couldn't take the girls out of Honduras without proper paperwork. We were all alone, with no one to help us.

Hotel in Tegucigalpa

Chapter 9

Early the next morning, there was a knock on our door. We opened it to find our lawyer and another man. Our lawyer looked disheveled and appeared to have been beaten up. The friend he had with him spoke fluent English. He explained what had happened, and why we were left to fend for ourselves and our children in this foreign land. He also informed us that when the police came to look for us in our room, we were gone. We had unknowingly escaped being detained and questioned along with the lawyer.

Evidently, someone in the hotel heard us talking about the children and the adoption. The fact that we were adopting two siblings raised a concern. This was created by false rumors about Americans taking Honduran children for organs to be transplanted into ill American children. This rumor spoke to the political times we were in with the Sandinista/Contra war and all the civil unrest throughout Central America. Despite the fact that the U.S. was helping in the war against Communism, we were considered the bad guys, and the stories they told about us were without truth or mercy.

When our lawyer checked us into the hotel and left to do our paperwork errands, someone called the police and reported him as trafficking children. This may explain why our hotel room was disturbed. They may have been searching for proof of this atrocious rumor that did not exist.

Upon his arrest, our lawyer was thrown in jail and was not permitted to call or contact us. We were unaware that we were being watched and followed by people at the hotel. The lawyer's friend explained that the lawyer was held overnight, our paperwork was confiscated and scrutinized by a judge, and one required paper was found to be missing from our file. The lawyer insisted that paper had been there and was convinced that the police removed it as a way of keeping him in custody. The next morning, a copy of the missing paper was obtained and was to be flown in from San Pedro to Tegucigalpa. Again we had to wait, as the paper was necessary for us to proceed to the Embassy.

At this point, we didn't know what to think or believe. I would be lying if I said the idea of just leaving the girls there and going home was not in our thoughts. We felt close to giving up and cutting our financial losses. We were exhausted. We just wanted to end this never-ending nightmare and go home. However, Maria's poor health and inability to function at her age level weighed heavily enough on our hearts and minds that we could not leave her to an uncertain future. The possibility that she would be placed into an orphanage with no chance of adoption would not allow us to give up.

*The future journey forward held more hope than the life
they left behind*

Chapter 10

The next morning, the lawyer returned with his friend and the missing paper. We gathered up the girls and our belongings, and proceeded to the American Embassy. We felt a huge sense of relief, knowing we would be dealing in English with Americans who would help us, give us a sense of security and be instrumental in getting all of us safely back to the U.S.

On our way to the Embassy, the lawyer informed us that they would drop us at the front door. His plan was to leave us, at that point, to fend for ourselves. After experiencing endless problems and challenges with his plan so far, we refused to give him the final lawyer fees unless he accompanied us into the office. We also demanded that he see us safely to the airport.

♡♡

Upon arriving at the Embassy, we were directed into a waiting room, while our lawyer was ushered into the office of the Consulate. After several minutes, we heard angry voices in both Spanish and English, along with what sounded like papers being thrown. The receptionist must have seen our panic and concern as she tried to comfort us, advising us to remain calm. She promised that we would soon be seen.

Again, our lawyer's friend was left to usher us into the office, and explain that the Embassy did not like the duplicate copy of the missing paper and wanted the original. The Embassy Officer was speculating that these children may never be ours and we were in a complete panic. This officer was berating our lawyer for doing a lousy job and telling him his shoddy work would not be tolerated by his office. The Embassy would not issue visas for the girls to come to the U.S. until the officer spoke directly with the judge who issued the adoption in San Pedro Sula.

We could tell that our lawyer, as well as his friend, were panicked and distraught. Again, the conversation became an angry mix of Spanish and English. We returned to the girls in the waiting room and tried to keep them occupied as we waited once again to learn our fate.

♡

After what felt like hours, our lawyer came out of the office and informed us that the issue with the missing paper had been resolved. We were then escorted back into the office to sign the proper paperwork for the girls' visas. Once everything was signed, the officer wished us good luck, gave us the visas and told us to go.

I hadn't been feeling well for several days with a stuffed head and a terrible earache, but there was no time to visit a doctor and obtain medication. We had a plane to catch, children to feed, a longing for our home country, and a small window of time to get to the airport.

After the lawyer dropped us at the airport in Tegucigalpa, I bought some aspirin for the pain in my ear and hoped this experience would soon be behind us. As we made our way to our gate, I prayed the girls would sleep through the flight and that I would not have any problems with the pressure changes or at least I could bear the ear pain that would surely come with takeoff and landing.

Again, we were on what seemed like the worst plane in the airport. The used and discarded planes the Honduran companies were buying from our country didn't seem fit to fly, but we didn't care. We just wanted to go home.

The flight home was painful, as I dug my hand tightly into my leg, trying to hold on. It was a relief that the pressure didn't seem to bother or affect the girls, and I was so grateful. The thought that we would soon be in Miami and on U.S. soil was what got me through the most painful earache of my life.

We were worried on our flight to Miami about going through Customs to get back into the U.S. We had heard horror stories from other adoptive parents about how disrespectfully they were treated upon arrival with their foreign adopted children. So, we were ready and prepared to fight. After all we had been through with the Honduran government and the political fallout, after all the problems, the patience required, the setbacks and the emotional rollercoaster, after all the adoption battles we were forced to fight and endure on foreign soil, we were ready to do battle on our own ground. By this time we were exhausted, but we were also adoption warriors with two little girls who needed to be healthy, cared for and loved. Our dedication to that responsibility, which we accepted as this adoption journey began, made us the fighters we needed to be in order to see this through.

We disembarked from that plane ready to do battle on familiar ground. We weren't doing patience and waiting anymore. We were going home! In our minds, we had one more struggle to get through at Immigration and we went in with an attitude of determination, ready to fight now on our terms.

There was a special immigration waiting area in Miami for parents arriving with adopted children. We handed over our paperwork, then realized the girls had diapers that needed to be changed. Just as we were finishing the diaper tasks, a woman came to us with our papers. Expecting a fight, we inquired as to what the problem was now. She appeared confused and quietly said that we were cleared to go. We could not believe this! Grateful as we were for this non-eventful entrance into our home country, we weren't quite sure what to do with the fight that was still in us.

Due to all the delays at the Embassy in Honduras and the rescheduled flights into Miami, we missed our connection back home. Because we wanted so desperately to be home, we tried to rent a car to drive the rest of the way. Unfortunately, there was some sort of huge convention in Miami and there were no rental cars available. We had no choice but to spend

the night in the Miami airport and take the first flight available
the next morning. There were also no available hotels near the
airport, so we set out for a closed-down bar at the far end of
the airport. There, airport security told us it would be quiet,
but that we would need to remain vigilant throughout the night
while the children slept.

Grateful for the airport security officer's advice, we
made our way to the deserted end of the airport. We found we
could fashion a type of protective crib by pushing two club-
shaped chairs together. Gary and I each draped ourselves over
their makeshift cribs and caught what amounted to cat naps
throughout the long night.

It was a long and exhausting night, but quiet and
uneventful. At one point, the security guard, who sensed our
exhaustion and stress when we missed our connecting flight,
came by to check on us. He instructed us to tell our story of
missed flights, the night in the airport and our adoption at the
ticket counter. We followed through with his advice in the
morning and the ticket agents placed us in first class for no
additional charge. Finally, something worked out in our favor.
We felt blessed and very grateful.

The flight back home allowed us to catch a 40-minute
nap. I noticed, although I felt dizzy and off-balance, my ear

did not hurt on this final leg of the journey. All that mattered was that we were going home. I knew my parents, my sister and her family would be awaiting our arrival at our home airport. That thought brought us so much comfort. Soon we would be home, where people cared about us and would help us recover from this entire ordeal. How grateful we were for their care and concern for us.

Just knowing we would have people we could count on was such a huge relief. Knowing that our grocery stores would be fully stocked was something we had taken for granted all our lives. In Honduras, there were empty shelves and many staples that were not available on a regular basis. I could hardly wait to turn on our faucets and be able to drink the water without boiling it!

Our homecoming was a celebration of balloons, posters and cheers, welcoming us and the girls to their new country. Our family must have spread the word among those waiting for other passengers, as the crowd erupted in cheers and shouts as we walked off the plane and into the terminal. Another adoptive family whose boys were adopted from El Salvador also came to the airport to greet us. It was a celebration of epic proportions. (Thirty-four years ago, before the tragedy of 9/11, people were free to be at the gate where family members arrived or departed. How things have sadly changed for all of us since then.)

At Last we arrived at our home airport

Chapter 11

The first few days at home were a blur. My dizziness continued and everything was off-balance. Although I could not walk correctly, the ear pain was gone, but it was almost impossible for me to focus. I was exhausted, and I could tell my mother was very worried about me. What a blessing it was to have her and my father there to help me take care of the girls when Gary immediately had to return to work. Gary had missed so much extra time from work that we had not counted on and our money had run out. I don't know how he went back to work so soon, as he was completely exhausted.

This entire experience had taken a huge toll on us physically, mentally, emotionally and spiritually. Never before had we felt so drained of energy and life, but we had two very needy special needs children to care for, and they had the best father a child could ever hope to get. So, Gary struggled forward one day at a time. Some days it was hour by hour, trying to recover ourselves, and meet the growing and constant needs of our daughters.

We were to face many challenges in the early days after we arrived back home. There were many issues with Carrie's adjustment to her new life. She was petrified of our dog and refused to be anywhere near her. We took turns alternating Carrie and "Rerun" in and out of the playpen. The poor dog was so confused, as Carrie would cry and scream whenever the dog came within a few feet of her. It would be weeks before Carrie could be in the same room with the dog without some sort of barrier between them.

Maria and Rerun, however, took to each other immediately and became best friends. Maria would allow the dog to lick her face, belly-laughing the entire time. She loved Rerun, and took advantage of every opportunity to touch and interact with her. Rerun truly loved Maria and her tail would wag with excitement each time Maria would wake from a nap.

Carrie had additional leftover issues from her short life in Honduras, where there was insufficient food and her belly was probably often empty. Somehow, the memory of her hunger triggered a habit to sneak and hide food. Each day when making her bed, I would discover hidden snacks of bananas and crackers. No amount of assurance about food would convince her to stop, so we regularly checked her hiding places. We had to be vigilant about attracting the bugs that were all too prevalent in the Florida climate. We never imagined back then that this would happen, or that it would take months of regular meals and snacks whenever she wanted them before this practice would slowly fade away.

$$\heartsuit$$

The first month at home was also a whirlwind of medical appointments and lab tests for the girls. They were much sicker than we thought and both were suffering from severe malnutrition. They were underweight, anemic, full of various parasites, and weak. We administered medications and took endless stool samples to the lab for repeated testing, which proved to be very expensive.

Unfortunately, health insurance at that time did not immediately recognize foreign adopted children as they did those born biologically. Perhaps the fact that foreign adopted children usually came with a host of medical issues factored into the fact that our health insurance company refused to cover the girls at all for the first six-month waiting period. Their health was too critical to try and wait that length of time to begin treatments, so the medical bills grew at an alarming rate.

It would be four months before we were able to totally eradicate the roundworms, tapeworms and other parasites that had already infested the children in their short lives. Carrie was the most infested while Maria recovered from that affliction much quicker, as her exposure in Honduras had been of less duration. It was shocking and heart-wrenching as Carrie's little body shed the huge worms that the doctor had not prepared us to encounter. It was little wonder that food would run through her and little nutrition was being absorbed by her body. Living in a clean environment, one cannot even imagine the atrocious parasites our Third World neighbors live with and endure.

The girls required numerous tests: several blood tests, TB tests, and tests we had never even heard of or knew existed. Gary and I were also given TB tests since we had been exposed to that Third World possibility. In addition, the pediatrician noticed and questioned my balance issues. After hearing our tale of the ear pain and plane ride, he examined my ears and informed me that the pain went away when my eardrum burst. I had ear infections in both ears. He was kind enough to prescribe medications and follow up with me until the infections were healed. There was nothing he could do about the permanent hearing loss, but within a short time, the dizziness was gone and my balance was restored. How thankful I felt for his kindness!

It was a major blessing six months later, when the waiting period for the health insurance passed and the girls were covered under Gary's medical insurance. We still had co-pays, but they were nothing like the "full pay" for doctors, lab tests and medications. We desperately searched for financial help, but there was nothing for which we qualified. The health department in our rural town was available to provide the girls with the many vaccinations they needed, and for that I was eternally grateful. It saved us from additional medical bills being added to our high-interest credit cards. We didn't know how else to pay the bills and get the children the care they desperately needed. So, we did the only thing we knew to do, and went into deep medical debt because of it.

At this point, funds were so low that I had to be very careful about using gas in the car. Gas was needed for the most urgent reasons: food shopping and medical care. There were times when I rolled pennies, put the girls in the double stroller my sister had bought me, and walked the mile to the corner convenience store for a loaf of bread.

Carrie and Maria's first summer in America

Chapter 12

Months flew by in a cyclone of activity. We were making little progress with the language barrier. The girls' building blocks of language were in Spanish, and English was presenting a confusing challenge for them. I tried to keep them bilingual with the limited Spanish I retained from my high school and college days, but it just wasn't enough.

I contacted the local school board and after hearing our story and predicament, they agreed to begin a course of speech therapy with both girls, even though they were so young. (Maria was two years old and Carrie was three.) In addition, I was invited into an early learning program, where I was able to make and create specific language and learning games geared toward increasing their intellectual and language development. This program offered childcare while I worked with teachers to create and design colorful and fun learning games that would help prepare the girls for a future preschool class.

The speech therapy was scheduled for twice a week, which helped fill our week between doctor appointments, trips to the beach and play dates at the local park. The girls were often ill, and it seemed someone was always trying to recover from something. Rarely were they both healthy at the same time. One of them was often down with various illnesses or viruses, so much time was spent at home treating symptoms. Their immune systems were so compromised, they caught every illness that blew by.

Fortunately, Gary wasn't around enough to catch all their ills. He had taken on a second job in an effort to tackle the huge medical debt weighing us down. The second income was a relief in that we could afford the extra gas to get to the learning center, doctor appointments and speech therapy. The down side to this was that I no longer had any relief from the 24/7 care and efforts required to juggle everything, but what a relief it was and I felt so blessed to have this great husband in my life. Gary would only see the girls on the weekends as he would leave for work very early each morning before they were up and return at night after they were asleep. Occasionally, the girls and I would pack a picnic dinner and meet him between jobs at a park in order to enjoy some family time together.

One day as Carrie ran down our hallway, she tripped and fell on the carpet, hurting her leg. She refused to stand and cried in pain. So, off to the emergency room we went. X-rays showed a green stick fracture in the growth plate in her leg, caused by the malnutrition she had suffered in Honduras. Our insurance company would only cover 80% of the bill and our credit card was just about maxed out. The bank refused our request for an additional extension to our credit. It wasn't our living expenses that were killing us financially, but the medical bills. We lived in a low-mortgage, doublewide mobile home on a raw piece of land that we were slowly clearing, so we were actually living below our means, except for all the medical bills.

At that point, I applied for and secured a job at the nearby convenience store where I often walked for bread. I was able to work the weekends, when Gary would be home to take care of the children. We did this for about four months until I became very ill and could no longer continue. After doctor appointments and several tests, I was diagnosed with mono and the Epstein Barr Virus. The doctor advised me to stop working because I could no longer function.

I was weak, completely exhausted and tired all the time. Taking care of the girls required every bit of energy I had. I remember crawling on my hands and knees into the kitchen to pull myself up to the counter so I could make the girls a sandwich for their lunch. It would be a few months before I would regain my strength and return to a full routine of all their therapies and appointments.

Chapter 13

It wasn't long after our return home that I began the long task of having the girls re-adopted in the States so they would have U.S.-issued birth certificates to replace their Honduran ones. Even though Florida was a state that recognized the international adoption, we had relatives living in other parts of the country whose states did not. If anything ever happened to us and the girls had to go live with these other relatives, their adoption could cause legal issues and be a problem for all concerned. We found an international adoption lawyer in Miami and once more began the process of adoption. This required additional paperwork, fees, another home study and travel to a court appearance in Miami.

Again, Gary took time off work and we planned what we hoped would be the final step in this long, stressful adoption process. Unlike Honduras, our adoption here in the States was relatively easy. It required a one-night stay in Miami prior to our meeting with the lawyer and our appearance before the judge in his chambers the next day.

It was a blessing that the girls were healthy during this process. We were dealing with a language we understood and a court system that at least made some sense. We were in and

out of the judge's chambers in a few short minutes with the
ability to receive a current birth certificate, and assurance that
the girls could go anywhere in the U.S. and their adoption
could not be questioned. The next step on our agenda was to
get them naturalized as U.S. citizens, which was required of us
by the court system at that time.

Shortly after the re-adoption, I began to write articles
for adoption magazines and support groups. I had majored in
journalism in college and had dreams of becoming a writer.
One article led to another and soon I received a call from
Cosmopolitan Magazine. They had read our adoption story
and wanted to feature our little family in a major project they
were doing on foreign adoption. We hesitated doing this but
finally agreed, after speaking with the editor. The article and
photographs appeared around the time we were in the process
of getting the girls through the court system to establish their
U.S. citizenship. In the 1980s, it required paperwork by the
adoptive parents and a formal appearance of the children in
court in order to be naturalized and awarded citizenship.

Following this court appearance, which was covered by the local newspaper, we were approached about an article they wanted to write. It was that article and my personal photographs that put me on the path to the writing career that I had dreamed about. Soon, I was writing for the newspaper, a business journal and other area publications. Life was good and I somehow managed to juggle the girls' needs, continue helping Gary to clear our land, and work as a freelance writer.

Naturalization Ceremony

Chapter 14

    The years before the girls were ready to start school full-time were a constant health, language and learning challenge. Despite the fact that we attended speech therapy classes several times a week, their language skills progressed very slowly. I continued to make and create learning games for them in a desperate effort to bring their development more on target for their age. Perhaps the early malnutrition played a bigger role in their struggles to move forward than we realized. I closely monitored their diets and allowed only healthy foods. It wouldn't be until they went to kindergarten that they would know about soda, cookies and candy. We tried to give them every advantage we could think of to rise above their early, unhealthy years.

    Maria finally learned to walk at 18 months. This was such a relief, as she was unable to even sit up by herself until she was 13 months old. She had a very large head and it always seemed to be a struggle for her to keep it raised. This concerned me, as she also seemed to have a large space at the bridge of her nose between her eyes. Carrie continued to cry a lot and had emotional outbreaks for what appeared to be no reason. I tried to watch for what might be triggering these outbreaks, but it was as if they came out of nowhere and nothing helped resolve them.

I questioned doctors about the issues with both of the girls but received no definite answers, only speculation. I was told that Carrie was spoiled and needed firm discipline, and not to react to her constant crying. It was suggested that Maria's large head and the spacing of her eyes was an inherited cultural appearance due to her Indian heritage. Issues with speech and learning continued, and became more evident once the girls were in elementary school. Preschool and the early language therapy provided only a glimpse into the challenges that would lie ahead.

The teachers were all very concerned with how delayed the girls were in their skillsets, learning and language. By the end of Carrie's first grade year and Maria's kindergarten, there was speculation that they would be better served in a special needs classroom. Gary and I rejected this idea because we wanted to give the girls more time to catch up to their peers. We also did not want them labeled at this early age. We felt strongly that they hadn't been given enough time to fully recover from their early health issues and malnutrition. So, I began to work with them daily and on weekends in areas where their teachers felt they needed the most additional help.

While I was covering school news for the newspaper, the principal of the girls' school suggested that I apply to become a substitute teacher. So, in addition to my writing, I took on occasional assignments to substitute teach grades K-2nd. This gave me an up-close and personal view of what needs were not being met. I also gained a lot of insight into special needs classes through subbing as an aide in these special classes.

What I learned was that I did not want my children to be labeled. At that time in educational history, it appeared that once children were labeled and placed in these classes, they were in them permanently and were not mainstreamed back into regular classes. I did not want this for my girls, so we struggled through years of working extra hours on education at home. The girls would complain about this, despite my efforts to make sure they had plenty of play time. We turned trips to the beach during the summer into fun educational opportunities and tried to disguise lessons into fun activities and adventures.

We always loved taking the family to the beach and playing in the shallow tide pools, where they could chase the small minnows that got stranded when the tides changed. Maria would run up and down the beach, pushing sand into the holes made by the crabs. When asked what she was doing, she proudly announced, "I am closing their doors so they don't come after me." Summers were carefree with many outdoor adventures, which always included watching for dolphins!

Written about our family days at the beach

I've seen a lot of beaches
and rode a lot of waves.
I've walked among the crystal sands,
collecting seashells that I saved.
I've fed crackers to the seagulls
and watched their graceful flight.
I've watched the porpoise play off shore
and released baby turtles at night.
I've stood upon a sandbar
and watched fish scurry around my feet.
I've traced the ripples left in the sand
where the ocean and shore meet.
I've been at the beach for sunrise
and drank my coffee at the shore.
I've witnessed many sunsets
and always long for more.
These simple treasures I have found
scattered along the way,
Have made my life worth living
and brought meaning to my days.
And now my children point and shout
at the porpoise swimming by.
They love to hunt for seashells
and watch the seagulls fly.
They love to run along the shore
and build castles in the sand.
Life here at the ocean's doorstep
is even better than we planned.
And the gift that I have given them
is an inherited legacy.
It's the reality of the dream,
my parents gave to me.

We all loved the beach, no matter what the weather

Chapter 15

Carrie was in second grade when she became ill a few weeks before Christmas. She complained of a severe headache, which the doctor diagnosed as a migraine. Despite rest and medications, several days went by with no improvement. Gary and I were panic-stricken! I either called or had her into the pediatrician every day for over a week. She would get a tiny bit better and then start to complain again of a headache. There was no fever or other symptoms, until the morning when she refused to get up. We could tell she was having problems speaking and couldn't even focus on answering our questions. Frantically, we put a call in to the doctor, who quickly responded to our call. Upon hearing how Carrie was acting, he instructed us to take her to the hospital immediately and he would meet us there.

Terrified beyond belief, but wanting to keep our fear from affecting Carrie, we got both girls ready and arrived at the hospital to find the doctor waiting for us. Testing began immediately. We knew it was serious when the doctor insisted we take Maria and go to get coffee at the other end of the hospital while they performed a spinal tap on Carrie. I know he could sense our overwhelming sense of helplessness and he didn't want us to experience the painful test they would need to do. He also didn't want Maria around close enough to hear Carrie's screams as they did what had to be done.

After several hours of testing, it was confirmed that Carrie had meningitis. The doctor said that he planned to begin IV antibiotics right away and he hoped she would be O.K. She would be hospitalized in the children's hospital and monitored closely, with constant tests throughout the day. Gary and Maria returned home to gather my things as I prepared to remain at the hospital with Carrie around the clock.

Gary adjusted his work schedule around getting Maria off to school each day. We were very concerned about the possibility of Maria contracting meningitis. The doctor warned us to be vigilant observing her, as it was a real possibility that she would contract meningitis from her close exposure to it.

As the days went by in the hospital, Carrie's improvement was very slow. At one point, I noticed that her eyes were now crossed, she was seeing double and often appeared confused. When I asked her to count to ten or say the alphabet, she could no longer get through the task correctly without my input or prompting. Something had gone seriously wrong in her brain and I was beside myself with worry. The doctor informed us that meningitis could have serious side effects. We had been through so much with these children that we were worn out, exhausted and heartbroken at this recent illness and the horrible toll it was taking on Carrie.

As Christmas approached, Carrie's blood tests and repeat spinal taps came back clear. She still had the residual effects of the meningitis, but the doctor was hopeful that they would eventually dissipate.

Carrie was scheduled to play Mary in a religious play at our church on Christmas Eve. She was released from the hospital two days before. Her eyes were still crossed and she was still seeing double. She was weak and often confused. The director of the play still wanted her to play the part and assured us that her lines were few and could even be left out, if necessary. Carrie very much wanted to play her role and be involved in the activity she had previously learned and practiced.

That Christmas play was an emotional one as Carrie, with her eyes crossed and not totally sure of herself, pulled off her role as baby Jesus's mother. Those who knew about her illness stood and clapped as the play came to a close. Not a dry eye in the place.

Fortunately for us and through the answer to many prayers, Maria remained healthy and never did contract meningitis. How blessed we were to once again rise above the challenges and struggles we encountered in our life's journey. Through the grace of God, forward we went.

Chapter 16

When Carrie returned to school after Christmas break, we soon learned that the residual effects of the meningitis, while not permanent, would take two years to fully overcome. She had lost the ability to remember anything that ran in a consecutive order. The alphabet, counting numbers, days of the week and months of the year were all abilities that would need to be re-learned. This would take time and patience. At the end of her second-grade school year, she was promoted to third grade, but the following year would prove to be a very tough and frustrating one.

Carrie's behavior throughout the next year had her teachers concerned and on edge. The school counselors were not equipped to deal with the issues and problems that continued, and we had no choice but to seek the professional help that she needed. She was angry, sad and acting out. We had to get her help. Again, the health insurance would only cover a portion of this therapy, and we fell deeper into medical debt. We were still trying to recover financially and pay all the bills from the meningitis and the hospital stay.

Once Carrie was in therapy, we learned that she had major issues with being adopted. We had always been very open with the girls about the fact that they were adopted. We emphasized that they were "chosen and special." We also altered their early story to protect them from learning some of the sad facts of how they were abandoned to starve by their young birth mother in the mountains. There was nothing to be gained by revealing the early truth, until it came up in therapy. Even then, we downplayed the role their birth mother played in their early health problems. The fact that Maria was, at one point, probably close to death from starvation was something we had kept from them until it was revealed in therapy.

At one point, Carrie told the psychologist that she wanted us to return to Honduras, find her birth mother and bring her back to the U.S. to live with us. This was a hard pill for us to swallow and we choked on the heartbreak of this for a very long time. Especially after the psychologist informed us that Carrie would probably never bond with us and would always blame me, her adoptive mother, for what her birth mother did by leaving them to starve in the mountains.

I didn't understand why I would have to suffer the brunt of her early circumstances. Surely the fact that we took the girls out of that situation, nursed them back to health, cared for them, loved them and sacrificed all we had could not be held against me. The therapist explained that Carrie's behavior issues stemmed from her early circumstances. She had no one in her life as a mother figure to blame except me, and she had to direct her anger on someone. Carrie had created this fantasy birth mother in her head who was perfect, never made her do schoolwork or anything else Carrie might not want to do. I would always pay the price for what the birth mother did to her by abandoning her.

This revelation by the psychologist stunned me. How do you continue to parent a child that feels so much anger and resentment toward you? We would never consider giving her back and returning her to Honduras, so we had to find a way to move forward and do the best we could with the unfair cards we had been dealt.

Fortunately, Maria didn't share her sister's feelings or issues. Our bond with Maria felt strong and would serve as the bandage that would allow us to continue parenting Carrie. I could not fathom ever separating these two sisters. We had already been through so much in our efforts to keep them together. Maria was the glue that keep us all together, at that time.

Christmas Holidays 1989

Chapter 17

The next few years were a series of behavioral issues with Carrie and learning challenges with both girls. Carrie would end up having to repeat third grade due to a mixture of her leftover meningitis issues, behavioral problems and suspected learning disabilities. It appeared that she might also be dyslexic. Whether this was biological or a result of the meningitis could not be determined. Nevertheless, we consulted several experts and were taught different techniques to help her work around her new challenges.

During this time, Gary lost his full-time job when the company he worked for relocated out of state and did not offer transfers to its employees. They were consolidating offices as well as services, and cutting the local staff completely. We were terrified with all the medical bills, not to mention our living expenses. Our personal overhead was low as we lived in a doublewide manufactured home in a rural area, but we were buried in medical debt. In addition, we were soon to be without family health insurance.

It was at this point that Carrie's therapy came to an end, when we could no longer afford to pay for it. We wrapped up therapy with the advice of the psychologist. We told Carrie that we would not consider finding her birth mother right now, but she would be able to search for her later in life, after she turned 18. If she wanted to find her badly enough, then this was her journey to follow and would not involve us. After this, Carrie's behavior seemed to improve. We also told her we could no longer afford to send her to the psychologist.

It took about three months of intense searching, but Gary finally found a decent job. The job paid less, but there was potential for advancement. We were just so grateful to have a steady income. The health insurance was not as good, but it was a huge relief to have insurance again and be able to take the girls to see the doctor when they needed it. We were blessed, though, during those few months of unemployment, that our family stayed healthy and we were spared additional medical bill worries.

Chapter 18

With the change in Gary's job, we had yet another new and different health insurance, which gave us a whole new set of doctors and medical experts to contend with. As I watched and measured the distance grow between Maria's eyes from year to year, I knew it was time to really push and insist on answers.

As Maria turned nine years old, I found a pediatrician who shared my concern. This doctor referred us to a geneticist at a children's hospital for an evaluation who ordered extensive testing, and the process was underway. I moved ahead with fear and trepidation, knowing something was not right and yet not sure I was ready to hear the answers.

Maria underwent extensive blood testing along with full body CT scans, skeletal surveys of bones throughout her body, full skull series X-rays and brain scans. Despite all the testing, there were no immediate answers. The geneticist asked us to be patient while she consulted her colleagues and experts in other facilities throughout the country. Patience was a word I really didn't want to hear or live by anymore, as it seemed to be a virtue that constantly alluded me.

In March 1993, after several months of testing and waiting, the geneticist called, wanting to see us. They were building an extensive file on Maria that several doctors wanted sent to a specialist in South Carolina at the Medical University. Getting definitive answers from the doctors was sketchy at best. No one wanted to venture a guess or share their thoughts at that time about Maria's condition.

After we agreed to comply with their request to send the file, additional bloodwork was ordered. They also took several rolls of film of Maria's face from all angles. This was all forwarded to the university, and patience once again became the main advice. They never advised us or told us what to do with all of our worry.

April passed quietly, and Maria seemed happy to avoid everything medical. She was tired of tests, doctors and hospitals. I felt so guilty putting her through so much, yet I somehow knew something was seriously wrong and that time was a factor. I knew it was up to me to push for the answers in order to secure her future. Perhaps we had a guardian angel that would not let me rest, poking me into always observing, thinking, wondering and pushing forward.

During this time, things began again to escalate with Carrie's emotional issues. It's possible that with the main focus on Maria, Carrie was feeling left out. She returned to counseling, which always seemed to bring out the worst in all of us. Carrie's emotional problems not only persisted, but grew worse. It was a very stressful and trying time for everyone.

Gary was working two jobs, trying to make a dent in the medical bills, and life was just overwhelming. In the midst of all this, a lump was discovered in my breast at my doctor's appointment and had to be addressed. Fortunately, after six months of regular testing, the problem resolved itself and I was so very grateful. Maybe all the stress was to blame for that. We were experiencing unending challenges and just prayed for better days ahead. We often thought of ourselves as clinging to the edge of sanity, and patience was our ultimate challenge.

Waiting rooms at medical offices became our second home

Chapter 19

Finally, in mid-May, Gary and I were called to meet with the geneticist who was compiling and directing Maria's case file. She was pretty sure she had a diagnosis for us. From the sound of her voice, I was pretty sure we wouldn't like it. Some things in life need no verbalization. At times, your heart can feel the tension vibrating in the air. This was to be one of those times.

When the nurse called our names to lead us to the conference room, I realized the crushing feeling in my chest was not only fear, but I was inadvertently holding my breath. I still remember the long silence that stretched before us in that sterile room as we waited for the doctor. Somehow the air just didn't feel safe, and neither did we. Maria's future hung in the balance.

I had promised God eight years earlier to love and protect her. The promise to love I was sure of. The promise to protect felt like it was slipping away. I was forever grateful that Maria was safe and far away from that hospital for the moment. I could keep my promise to protect her for at least a while longer.

As the doctor entered the room, I sensed that she brought with her an end to innocence in Maria's young life and a challenge to parenthood that I only dreamed of in my worst nightmares. I must give the doctor credit for handling herself in the most professional way. She took her time and gave us plenty of information, or at least as much as she thought we could medically and technically understand.

This doctor, along with a few other medical experts, diagnosed Maria with a very rare genetic disorder called craniometaphyseal dysplasia. This disease caused an unusual amount of bone to build up in the skull area and long bones of her body. When that happens, the narrow opening in the skull which permit the nerves to travel between the brain and outer skull can become filled in with bone. If the nerves become depressed, blindness, deafness and paralysis can result. As if that wasn't frightening enough to imagine, the possibility of water collecting on the brain and other serious complications were added to the list. The long bones in her arms and legs would also be affected, as well as her jaw and the passageways necessary for breathing.

The doctor apologized for giving us such detrimental news. When we asked for some printed materials or books about the disease, the bomb we were not expecting dropped.

So little was known about this condition that nothing had been published. A colleague of this doctor in Charleston, South Carolina had confirmed the diagnosis, and wanted to see and study Maria. Dr. Lyndon Key, a pediatric endocrinologist, was one of the original founders and researchers of the disease. The disease was so rare that there were no statistics and the disease, more common in boys, was very rare in girls.

An eye exam for Maria was immediately scheduled. Due to the widening space between her eyes that had always worried me, the doctor was concerned that she could already be suffering from impaired vision and not be aware of it. We were blessed and so fortunate when her eyes tested normal. What a gift this good news was for us. We were coming off a month of repeated bad news and desperately needed something positive to cling to.

Throughout the Spring, Carrie continued to attend therapy sessions, but we saw little progress. We felt it was a huge waste of our time, energy and resources, but nevertheless we continued. We just wanted to see her happy and well-adjusted. We felt like no progress was being made, but it wasn't for lack of trying. Juggling the stress of Maria's medical condition and Carrie's emotional issues kept us putting one foot in front of the other as we struggled through the days and weeks that followed.

In early June, I spoke with Dr. Key in Charleston and agreed to an appointment on June 25th that would also include a consult with a pediatric neurosurgeon, Dr. Bruce Storrs. Dr. Storrs had worked with bone reconstruction at the Toronto Children's Hospital. Although he was listed among the top five surgeons in the country, in some ways he was the last person we wanted to have to meet. In the conversation with Dr. Key, he also recommended putting Maria on an experimental therapy drug which would hopefully help her bone-building to stabilize. At the time, I thought he was crazy. Experiment on my daughter? And neurosurgery? My attitude then was, "Prove it, convince me."

June 25th dawned as a beautiful sunny day as we drove to South Carolina. Maria seemed oblivious to the turmoil that I thought was all too obvious, so we evidently did a good job of faking it. In her mind, we were going on an adventure. Carrie was home with family members, so we were free to focus totally on Maria's appointments.

Our first appointment was with the neurosurgeon, Dr. Storrs. He answered all our apprehensive, challenging questions calmly, and then went out of his way to connect personally with Maria. He recommended surgery to reconstruct Maria's nose and forehead, plus widen any opening in the skull where nerves pass through. These passages were narrowing and in time would completely fill in with bone, causing loss of eyesight and hearing, along with facial paralysis. He described this grueling procedure in detail. Although this was his everyday world, it clearly wasn't ours.

Throughout our time with this surgeon, I came to realize how passionate he was about helping and saving children. As a father himself, I think he had an idea of how we felt. He knew he could give Maria a chance at a normal life with increased self-esteem. She had already been made fun of in school for her unusual facial features and her feelings seemed very important to him. This went a long way in earning our faith and trust in him.

By our next appointment with Dr. Key, most of our
questions had been answered and our fears addressed as much
as possible. However, we asked the same questions all over
again. I wanted to be sure everyone was in agreement with the
same plan, as I looked for discrepancies everywhere I could.

By the time our appointments were over, we had a
prescription for calcitriol, fear in our hearts, but relief that
these doctors really appeared to be Maria's best chance for a
normal life. We were also aware that Maria had a 50% chance
of passing the condition onto her own children. In addition,
the disease was extremely rare in girls. Seems we won some
unfortunate lottery that left Maria's health and future
uncertain.

While the disease was not fatal for certain, some
children did not live into adulthood. One thing was for sure:
none of us would ever be the same again. It's strange how you
can point to moments in time and know exactly when it felt
like the ground disappeared from under you. How well those
moments teach you appreciation and gratitude for the little
blessings in life.

After additional tests were completed on Maria, her
pediatrician informed us that the disease was beyond the scope
of her expertise and we would be referred to the care of a

pediatric endocrinologist, going forward. So, we waited for that referral and anticipated another round of tests and explanations.

Meanwhile, throughout June, Carrie continued with therapy, which was a one-hour drive each way. Between everyone's appointments, we spent days in the hot car, which had no air conditioning, and therapy became more of an unpleasant task and challenge for all of us. Carrie didn't want to go there any more than we did, but we were determined to do all we could to help her.

Carrie at Easter

Chapter 20

July was a busy month, with trips to the new pediatric endocrinologist. Dr. George Bright was a wonderful grandfatherly type doctor who was very interested in Maria. He wanted to make certain that she understood her condition and explained it all to her in a simple but straightforward manner. He explained that the bones in her body had special rules to follow, just like she did in school. The problem was that her bones needed some medication and other procedures to help them do what they were supposed to do. Maria appeared to easily understand and accept his explanation. My heart was bursting with gratitude toward this grandfatherly doctor, who took the time to explain the disease to Maria in a way that was neither horrendous nor intimidating for her. I thanked God for leading us to this wonderful man.

It is not easy, as other parents know, to turn your child over to the care of another individual, but that day, I found in Dr. Bright the compassion and, most importantly, the guts to do what was best for an individual child and let the politics of health insurance be damned. Here was a doctor who put safety and ethics as his number one priority. He was as outspoken about the medical and insurance system as I was, but coming from a member of the medical community, I knew it proved he was honest and would fight for the best for our child.

Additional testing was then done on Maria's kidneys as well as clinical tests to confirm that she still had full control of feeling throughout her facial muscles. All this was done in an effort to establish baselines before she was put on the experimental medication. The medication was to be administered as soon as the doctor could get permission from the medical board to treat her. We would then have to sign release forms for the medication. Because the disease was so rare, all treatments, clinical results and her patient file were to become part of the research. What they would learn from Maria would benefit children who would be diagnosed with the disease in future years.

In late July, authorization finally came through for Maria's neurosurgery, and the lengthy scheduling process began. School would begin soon and we were battling a major timeframe with the surgery. The experimental medication authorization also came through and we learned that the insurance company refused to pay for it. The calcitriol would cost us $1,200 for a one-month supply and the doctors expected her to be on this protocol for at least six months, in the hope that it would stabilize the bones in her face and skull following the surgery.

The medical bills were piling up from both girls, as Carrie still continued with therapy to address behavior and learning disabilities. Financially, we were in way over our heads. I was unable to work due to all the medical appointments, plus I had no one to watch the girls. It was a blessing that my mother offered to come stay for a while and help us through Maria's surgery.

Gary was rarely home from working two jobs and I was so very lonely. My mother's company and moral support was a lifeline for my sanity. I was so grateful to have another adult to keep me company through the long days. I will be eternally grateful for her tremendous support, love, concern and her mere presence. She is now an angel who looks down on me often and I miss her every day of my life.

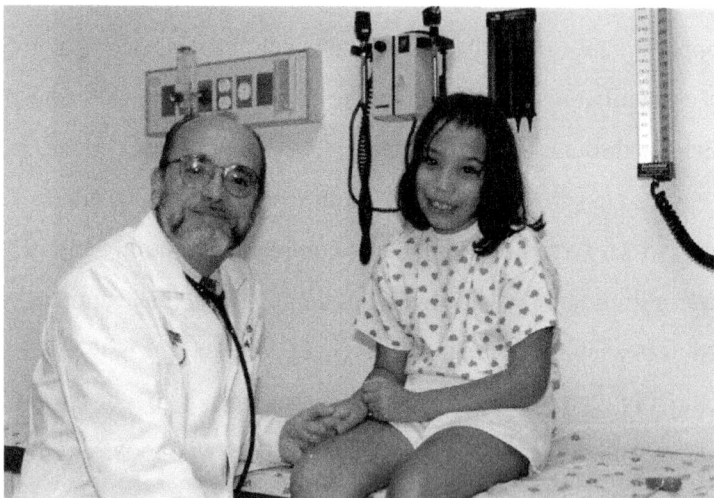

Dr. Bright and Maria

Chapter 21

August was another hectic month, getting ready for school. Carrie received a referral to be tested at a speech and language center, but could not get in until October. Her issues continued and at times escalated to new levels. She didn't consider me her "real" mother and had created a fantasy birth mother who was perfect in every way. She rarely passed up an opportunity to throw it in my face that I was not her real mother. In her eyes, I was never good enough.

The therapist felt she had not bonded with us and there was a good chance that she never would. Still, we continued onward, praying for her attitude and the situation to resolve itself in some way. The expense of therapy continued to be an enormous financial burden and the excess stress of the situation was ripping us apart. No healing was taking place and at times, we succumbed to feeling hopeless.

Maria was admitted to the Medical University of South Carolina for surgery on August 26th. Dr. Storrs, the neurosurgeon, would be opening the surgery, assisted by plastic surgeon Dr. Warren Gould, along with Dr. Key. Together, these doctors would reshape Maria's forehead and nose, and open wider any areas of the skull where crucial nerves would need to pass. She would have a large incision from ear to ear and over the top of her head. The skin covering her face would be peeled back. Her hair would be shaved and the bone beneath her skin reconstructed.

Since the Medical University of South Carolina is a teaching hospital, Maria was on display and of particular interest to many medical professionals who had never encountered this rare disease. She seemed to take these group visits in stride and the doctors kept their word that she would not be in any way traumatized by all the activity around her.

That first afternoon and evening after Maria was admitted, we made our way down the hall to the playroom. This was an amazing area of bright colors, creative activities and plenty of other children for Maria to play with. Many of the children arrived in wheelchairs, wagons and on foot, trailing their IVs, oxygen masks and various other types of medical equipment. Some were undergoing chemo and radiation, some were bald, but all of them were smiling. This was a very humbling experience, but there was to be no sadness in this room. This room was designed to let the patients be children, and enjoy all the fun and activities their healthy peers were able to enjoy on a daily basis.

The next morning, Maria was given a sedative by mouth, which kept her calm and sleepy. I couldn't help thinking that maybe the wrong person had been sedated and it should be the parents who get these sedatives. When they came to take Maria to surgery, we kissed her and told her we would see her later. We forced ourselves to act as if we were sending her out to the bus for another day at school. We were led to a waiting room, which was filled with other stressed faces, for the predicted two to three hours of surgery.

Three hours turned into five hours, and we were very worried. Finally, we were called to the pediatric intensive care unit, where Maria was just waking up from surgery. As we entered the recovery area, we recognized the well-bandaged face was actually our daughter. The doctors had prepared us well for her post-surgery appearance. Tears filled my eyes to see her bloodied, swollen, discolored face, but she was breathing on her own and alive. The surgery was more extensive than originally anticipated and took several hours longer for the reconstruction, but it was a huge relief to have this part behind us.

I had many discussions and pep talks with Maria prior to her surgery. We had discussed a plan that if she came out of surgery too tired to talk, I would squeeze her hand. I told her, "If you are O.K., squeeze my hand back and that will be our secret code." I held my breath and squeezed her hand very gently, not sure she would remember or respond. I felt her fingers begin to move: first a gentle squeeze, followed by one big strong one. Tears of relief and joy flowed down my face!

We passed the remainder of the day with Maria throwing up and sick to her stomach from the anesthesia. We held her hand, her head, her bowl. It was hard to see her feel so awful, but we stayed by her side long into the night until the throwing up finally stopped, thanks to the medication the doctors ordered. We managed to get three hours of rest and woke to Maria waiting for us with brighter eyes. She was watching a video, eating Jell-O and complaining that she was hungry. She complained to anyone who would listen, and told the first doctor who arrived that the people taking care of her were starving her. He found this amusing and immediately ordered her a full tray of food. Her recovery after just a few hours was impressive and we were so very thankful.

The day of Maria's surgery and for two days following, a hurricane was threatening our home where my mother and sister were taking care of Carrie. We were terrified for them and thankful when the hurricane by passed our home area. But now, we were in harm's way in South Carolina, with a child just out of surgery. The hurricane forced the hospital to discharge us two days after Maria's surgery, as an evacuation order had been declared for the South Carolina coast. It was a tense drive home as we were not sure what weather or evacuation traffic we might encounter. However, we must have had a guardian angel along for the ride because we arrived home safely, despite all the traffic.

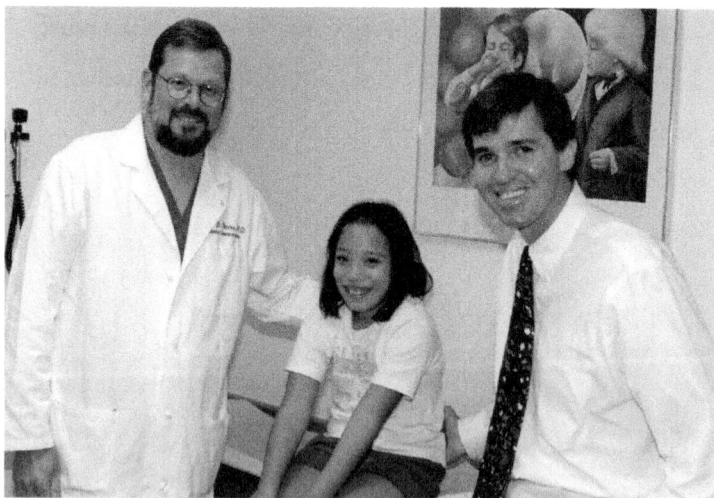

Maria with her surgeons

Chapter 22

The days following our return home were quiet as Maria quickly recovered. Her appetite was good, and we were all able to get some desperately needed sleep and rest. Carrie was thrilled to have everyone back home. She missed Maria terribly and went out of her way to be helpful, which gave us some much-needed hope for the future.

Six days later, Maria's stitches and bandages were removed by Gary on our back porch. I think of this now and just cringe. Due to the circumstances of the hurricane, we were left without the doctors to remove them. There were no medical professionals in our area willing to do this for liability reasons, and directed us back to South Carolina. Dr. Gould walked us through the task over the phone and it worked out fine.

Maria was able to return to school after missing only seven days. Her incision was covered and protected by wide multi-colored headbands, which reduced the trauma and the questions from her fifth-grade classmates. Now with her eyes closer together and her forehead reconstructed, she would not have to endure unkind taunts and name-calling.

In Mid-September, we traveled back to South Carolina for a recheck with the doctors. They were very pleased with Maria's results and arranged for her follow-up treatments to be handled locally by Dr. Bright, so we would not have to travel. This made it much easier for us to meet the needs of both girls without the added travel expense.

At this point, we decided to cease Carrie's behavioral therapy and concentrate on the results from the Speech and Hearing Center, where they identified some of the learning issues that possibly were contributing to Carrie's frustrations and emotional outbursts. Carrie hated school, and was unhappy and frustrated throughout her school days. I received numerous calls from her various teachers about her disruptive and stubborn behaviors. I began to wonder if her learning, speech and hearing issues were a large part of the problem.

Testing revealed the extent of Carrie's language disability and the way her brain processed information. The Speech and Hearing Center emphasized the importance of giving her small bits of information at a time to deal with in order to cut down on her feelings of being constantly overwhelmed. Processing information was a huge obstacle for her, and the behavioral therapy and counseling was not helping. We had had enough disruptions in our lives and were anxious for things to find some form of "normal."

That same evening, "normal" was to elude us once again. I fell while out in the shed and the next day confirmed a broken right foot and shoulder. It was all just so hard to believe. Life had finally settled down—or so we thought.

Mom was always there for us

Chapter 23

October began with a full cast on my leg, an immobilizer on my arm and a wheelchair in order to get around. My precious mother, who was ready for her return trip to her home state, cancelled her flights and made arrangements to stay an extra two weeks to help me. Once again, she came to our rescue and I was so grateful to have her help and especially her company. I was in a lot of pain and very limited in what I was able to do.

Maria had an appointment with Dr. Bright in early October and he recommended that she be seen by an orthodontist. She continued with the experimental medication, as we watched our credit card balance grow. We called the manufacturer of this medication, with no luck in getting free samples or having the cost covered. My sister worked for a local doctor who was able to get us a "one-time" free sample, and we were grateful for the one month we didn't have to come up with the $1,200.

My mother left for her home at the end of October and we all hated to see her go. We could have never done all that had to be done without her help and there were no words adequate enough to express our gratitude. Out of the worst of times, we reaped the blessings of special moments that will stay with us forever. My mother was the perfect example of what every mother should be and I am so proud to be her daughter.

♡

November was a fairly quiet month as the girls were both back on a regular school and activity schedule. There were a few appointments, but they were more routine and nothing like the constant ones we had been encountering. The cast came off my leg and the wheelchair became a distant memory. I was cautioned about not driving since our car was a manual transmission, but I was determined to drive in order to get myself and the girls around. Besides, I had no choice. There was no one to help me. I was referred to physical therapy three times a week and had to get back on my feet. So, I plunged forward with exercise and walking.

December arrived with Christmas on the horizon, so it was an exciting time for the girls. Maria continued to be monitored with blood tests and 48-hour urine cultures. She began having hearing issues and was found to have bilateral ear infections, which required several rounds of antibiotics.

Carrie's behavior actually improved with the end of counseling and we focused on addressing her learning disabilities. I felt that this new approach was helping to alleviate some of her educational stress of which we were previously unaware.

The holiday break from school was a welcome relief for all of us. There were no appointments or testing. We were able to enjoy more family play time and loved the simple activities most families take for granted. It was a time of beach walks, shark tooth hunting, seashell collecting and playgrounds.

Soon it was January (1994) and school was back in session. The new year ushered in more ear problems and infections for Maria. Three heavy doses of antibiotics still had not resolved her problems. Hearing loss was evident and we were fearful that the surgery might not have opened the nerve canals in her skull wide enough.

In mid-January, Maria saw a maxillofacial surgeon for evaluation. It appeared that her disease had caused the bones in her skull to absorb the extra calcium that would have formed some of her adult teeth. In other words, she was missing adult teeth, and some of her baby teeth needed to be retained. This surgeon recommended orthodontics followed by a surgery to reposition and reconstruct her jaw. Yet another obstacle for Maria to face, along with another expense for us, as much of this would not be covered by insurance. It was amazing the lengths that the health insurance company would go to in order to get out of covering craniofacial diseases and the issues that resulted from them. We were not the only family facing their excuses, as these results resonated throughout the cranial facial support community.

The welcome news came at the end of the month, when Dr. Bright determined it was time to remove Maria from the experimental protocol. He would follow closely to monitor her, but for now, Maria was free to return to a regular diet and she was thrilled. While on the calcitriol medication, it was important for her to not consume any milk or dairy products. This included pudding, pizza, milkshakes and ice cream, which were her favorites. That night, she chose to celebrate with pizza and ice cream.

Chapter 24

The next few months passed quietly, medically speaking. Carrie settled down a bit more and I was no longer getting negative phone calls from her teachers. She was being much more co-operative around the house and helpful, even when I didn't ask her. It was such a blessing to see her happier and interacting as a member of the family. I had high hopes that the worst was behind her, as she was doing better in school. We continued to follow the advice from the learning experts and Carrie no longer hated school.

Maria, however, continued to experience hearing loss and was referred to an ear, nose and throat specialist. He recommended ear plugs for showering. If the problem persisted, she would have tubes surgically implanted in her ears. It was possible that the middle ear bone could be checked for any sign of the dysplasia associated with her disease. In April, Maria was put on yet another round of antibiotics for ear infections. Dr. Bright encouraged us to see another surgeon about reconstructing Maria's chin, which was building excess bone, and moving forward with the orthodontia.

Our health insurance had changed once again and the doctors in South Carolina were no longer an option. However, there was another craniofacial surgeon in our home state of Florida who was known to have some experience with the disease. Dr. Mutaz Habal, who saw this disease in his homeland of Cuba, came highly recommended. Again, we waited for the insurance company to approve the referral so we could set up an appointment.

Prior to the appointment with Dr. Habal, Maria had molds taken of her ears and custom ear plugs made. This required a small surgery that took nine minutes and she was back to school the following day. The custom ear plugs would allow Maria to shower and swim. They were guaranteed not to leak and would hopefully keep fluid out of her ears, thus eliminating further infections. She had been on constant antibiotics for months and we were anxious for her to continue without them.

During this time, we received a call from FACES, a craniofacial foundation out of Chattanooga, Tennessee. We had applied to this foundation months prior as the medical bills grew, hoping they could somehow help us or refer us to somewhere that could. Now, they had accepted Maria as a client. This meant they would help cover our travel expenses to facilities over 100 miles from our home, in addition to food and lodging. This might not sound like a lot after all we had been through, but it would be a tremendous help for our travel to see Dr. Habal in June, when school was out for the summer. This organization was so supportive and we became a resource for them as well, with this unusual and rare disease.

Soon, we were hearing from social workers, doctors and families who were seeking information as a few other children were being diagnosed. Families were calling us for information about our doctors and hospitals. A few calls came from immigrant families. Some calls came from as far away as Mexico and Canada. One immigrant family had been traumatized by all the white-coat doctors who did not speak Spanish gathered around their 14-year-old daughter and they fled back home to Mexico, refusing further treatment. Those calls would go on periodically for years, as more children were diagnosed. If our experiences with Maria's disease could help someone else, then we were glad to share whatever information we could to help.

Also, FACES would use Maria's case and our experience as an example of the problems with healthcare in this country when they appeared before the U.S. Congress. We were willing to travel to Washington, D.C. and appear with this organization in an effort to provide fair healthcare coverage for these special needs children.

As time moved forward, Carrie continued to improve in a variety of areas. She was rarely ill and it was such a blessing to have her attending and waiting patiently in countless waiting rooms for Maria's appointments. The school year was winding down and Carrie was happily looking forward to summer. She was smiling more, crying less and acting as though she liked me, or at least tolerated me.

School let out and in early June we began another round of medical appointments. Maria had ear tubes surgically inserted and her hearing re-checked. Everything was in place and it all looked good, despite the fact that she still suffered some hearing loss. Since the tubes were not successful at restoring her full range of hearing, the doctor felt the loss was due to a slight compression of the audio nerves from the craniometaphyseal dysplasia. Fortunately, the hearing loss was not yet substantial enough to warrant medical intervention, but would need to be re-evaluated every six months.

The girls were so glad to be out of school for the summer, and not too happy with my summer homeschooling plan to keep them learning and tackle some of the curriculum they would encounter in the 6th grade. I wanted to give Carrie a head start on the next school year by introducing her to new skills in the small quantities recommended for her learning disabilities. I knew Carrie was smart. It was the learning disability and not her intelligence that was the issue.

In mid-June, we traveled to see Dr. Habal, who treated children with Maria's disease in his Cuban homeland. During this appointment, the doctor explained how he had reviewed all of Maria's tests and her entire medical file. It was his opinion that Maria's disease had progressed past the point of any further surgical intervention. The additional testing he had done determined that the bone in her skull was so thick that any further surgery could shatter her skull, causing terrible damage. She was also at risk of suffering a collapsed trachea during any surgery.

He explained that, "The train for certain forms of medical intervention has left the station." The time to address the dental situation was upon us and possibly also past. He cautioned that we needed to keep her as healthy as possible because there was no further opportunity to medically intervene if she would ever need a cranial shunt. Any further surgery could cause her trachea to collapse and her airways were subject to be crushed. This was quite a shock to us, as we came to realize that her life of surgeries and medical intervention had reached their limit.

While this was good news in that she would no longer be subjected to all these interventions, it also left us terrified for what this might mean for her future. If there was nothing they could do for her, the rest of her life was fully in God's hands. In some ways, that news was almost harder to hear and accept than anything we had ever heard so far. Maria was so tired of all the medical tests and appointments that I think she was happy to think they were coming to an end of sorts. It would mean returning to some form of a normal life which she seemed to welcome, heading into middle school.

Summer passed with many dental appointments. Maria saw oral surgeons, dental reconstructive specialists and orthodontists. Since her system didn't have enough calcium properly distributed in her body, she was missing several adult teeth. The plan was to try and retain a few of her baby teeth. Once the remaining teeth were in place after braces, she would still require at least one partial plate. The bone in her jaw was too thick to allow implants.

The next three years would be a series of adjustments to her braces as well as the overall dental plan. Some baby teeth were not holding up and could not be retained. Eating certain foods was a challenge and others were eliminated from her diet. The plan was that before she was out of high school her braces would be off, her partial plates would be in place and she would have a beautiful smile, despite a very long and expensive process.

High school graduation

Carrie

Maria

Chapter 25

The new year in 1995 arrived promising a quieter life. Throughout the last year, Maria had been to over 48 medical appointments in an effort to accomplish as much as possible while the window of opportunity was open. The doctors all seemed to be in agreement that they had done all they could for her. Further intervention would not work in her favor and had the potential to cause her more harm. They felt she needed to be watched and monitored on a year-to-year basis, but were open and honest that if an issue with the disease arose, there was probably little they could do about it or to correct it. Maria was in God's hands now and while we were anxious about the future, we also felt at peace, knowing we could now return to a normal life. A higher power than all of us was now in charge of the rest going forward.

By the time life was to settle down, we were so deeply in debt that Gary working two jobs could no longer make a dent in the leftover medical bills. I was trying to help with my freelance writing, but the money we needed was just not there. I had gone to college to study journalism and writing was my dream, but it just wasn't working for our family or finances. Our credit card was maxed out and the interest was eating us up. At that time, the company Gary worked for was hiring and needed someone with a strong English background. While the thought of giving up my dream was heart-wrenching, I knew it was the right thing to do.

It was a matter of survival, and I knew the choice to go to work full-time would eventually prove to be worth it. It would mean that our story, this book, would become impossible to write. I had kept a detailed journal of our family journey, so I knew the story would always be retrievable. With a heavy heart, I accepted the full-time job. It would be over twenty-five years before this book would be written.

There is something to be said for challenges and obstacles that bind a family together. There was nothing more we could do for Maria medically, and it was time for the girls to live a more normal middle school and high school life. Many of the medical changes that had, for so long, bonded us all together seemed to be somewhat resolved. As we focused on the girls' typical teenage years of academics, proms, drivers licenses and working part-time jobs, we found the bonding challenges turning into competitive issues between the girls.

As a parent knows, the teen years of parenting are not for the faint of heart. Being only 11 months apart, there were constant issues between the girls that were unable to be resolved. Nothing we did or said could mend their grievance with each other. Their once close, supportive bond deteriorated in a heartbreaking way. Our early struggle and determination to keep these two sisters together seemed to have failed and it was a very bitter pill to swallow. Sadly, this estrangement continued through adolescence into adulthood. The best we can hope for is that time will be kind, resolve all issues and heal all wounds.

The teen years with Dad

Chapter 26

So, where did we all go from there with our lives?

Today, as I write this, the high school and college years are far behind us. The girls finished their various educations and moved on into adulthood. They have been blessed in countless ways and have overcome obstacles most children do not face.

Although Carrie struggled through her school years with learning disabilities, she managed to find ways to compensate for them and succeed. She attended a career institute and became a veterinary technician. We often reflect back on the small toddler who was so terrified of our dog that we had to keep them separated for weeks. Now, though, her love of animals is her passion and she has found her calling in life with them. She lives happily in another state with her boyfriend and their four dogs.

Maria, who the doctors in Honduras advised us against taking, graduated college with a bachelor's degree in Math. She attended college on a Bright Futures scholarship that she worked very hard to achieve during her high school years. Her dental work was completed in her senior year of high school, in time for her to be smiling large in her senior graduation photos.

Despite all of Maria's medical challenges, she is very gifted in her ability to design business systems. She continues to face medical issues and challenges that she must consistently monitor, but she is relatively healthy at this time and onto a journey of her own.

We are very pleased that the girls are hard workers. They have carved out a life of their own making and seem to be self-reliant at this time. We hope their journey forward will be filled with much love, success and happiness.

Thankfully, as the years passed, the medical bills were paid and the financial burdens lifted. Gary and I were fortunate that our income remained lucrative and stable, until we were financially secure. As the company we worked for phased out the long-term employees, we transitioned into retirement, and trained two Shih Tzus who went on to become therapy dogs. Together with Isla and Tootles we visit nursing homes, homeless shelters and other facilities as requested. I guess you could say that our lives have "gone to the dogs." It is a very good and rewarding endeavor. Thank you, Isla and Tootles, for saving us.

Reflections

The girls, in many ways, have been given everything they need to make a successful life for themselves. They have been blessed to be raised in an extended family that accepted them unconditionally. Our extended families have always loved and cherished them. They were educated in a school that welcomed them as the first Hispanic students in the school system. The school provided additional language therapy and more, so that the girls were able to catch up to their peers.

Although much has transpired recently in our country over immigration, we doubt that either one of the girls will ever fully understand or appreciate the gift this country has been for them. While others from their birth country cross many miles of unrelenting heat and dangerous terrain in the hopes of becoming American citizens, our daughters are blessed with citizenship and an American life that their adoption provided. We, as parents, are so very grateful for the extended family and community that embraced them.

We hope in the future that our children will give back to the world some of the good that was bestowed upon them, by being a blessing to others. We strongly believe in kindness, volunteering and being a beacon of light in this world for those less fortunate. If our efforts to "nurture" is to gift us with a feeling of accomplishment, then any and all sacrifices we have made will pay it forward through our daughters. We couldn't ask or wish for anything more.

It is often said, "Life is a journey, not a destination." How often we pause along the way and look back on where we have traveled. The past cannot be changed, and so we journey forward into the uncertainty and possibilities of the future. Perhaps the best part of the journey lies in who we choose to walk beside us. Those who travel alone are somewhat limited to the creativity and curiosity of a solo experience. A joint venture insures many varied experiences and a path of unimaginable possibilities. Life has a flow of its own, and those seeking peace are wise to accept where the flow transports them. Writing this book has helped me come to terms with where all our lives are today.

This is a story of lives changed by adoption. A story of hopes and dreams of a life of purpose and fulfillment. It's also been said that, "Life happens while you are busy making other plans." So it was with this adoption and even now going forward, with the journey ahead and beyond.

Namaste.

About the author

Patti originally self published a book of poetry back in 1990. Today, she works once again as an author and free lance writer.

She lives in northeast Florida with her husband and their two therapy dogs, Isla and Tootles. This therapy team volunteers in nursing homes, homeless shelters, and various other facilities when requested. Their leisure activities include camping, beach walks and other dog-friendly adventures.

She loves hearing from readers and can be reached at tootlesisla@gmail.com.

Isla and Tootles working at Gracie's Kitchen

Printed in Great Britain
by Amazon